Tiger
in your
Living Room

Contents

Written by Inbali Iserles

Collins

1 Here kitty, kitty …

There are 500 million pet cats around the world. That's a lot of fluff! Today, cats are much-loved members of the family. But this was not always the case – once upon a time, all cats were wild, from **majestic** tigers to tiny, rusty-spotted cats. So how did these **fearsome** hunters become the friendly **felines** we know so well?

We will try to solve the puzzle by looking at paintings, bones and other **evidence**. It's time to sharpen our claws and step out on an adventure. We are off in search of the first pet cats …

Cats have made a home in our houses and in our hearts.

What are cats?

Pet cats – also known as "**domestic** cats" – are part of the cat family, along with big cats like lions, cheetahs and panthers. All cats are brilliant hunters that share a common **ancestor** from ten to 15 million years ago. As the first human ancestor lived around four million years ago, this makes cats much older than us!

Furry facts

The world's biggest cats are Amur tigers. A single Amur tiger can stretch to three metres from nose to tail, and weigh up to 300 kilograms. That's as long as a small car and as heavy as five adult humans!

The world's smallest cats are rusty-spotted cats. One rusty-spotted cat can measure as little as 50 centimetres, including the tail. Kitten-sized when full-grown and weighing only about one kilogram, this cat could sit in the palm of your hand.

2 The perfect hunter

What do all cats have in common?

- Cats are **carnivores**: they must eat meat to survive.
- They have excellent hearing, sight and smell – perfect for hunting.
- They have retractable claws that they tuck away when not in use. Cheetahs are the only cats whose claws do not fully retract. The added grip helps them run faster.
- Most wild cats are **solitary** – they live on their own. Lions are the only cats that live in family groups.

Pet cats have learnt to live with us.

What makes pet cats special?

Dogs are often thought of as loyal. Pet cats are more **independent** than dogs, but unlike wild cats, our pet cats are not completely solitary. They live happily with humans and enjoy our company. Some will live with other cats – or even dogs!

Furry facts

Scientists have discovered that most cats care if their owners are around. Cats see us as their "carers", much as a kitten might look upon its mother.

Come closer, my pet …

So how did cats become tame? We can begin to solve the puzzle by looking at evidence, like old bones. They tell us that cats and people lived near to each other in **prehistoric** times, but they did not live together. During the day, humans hunted or found fruit, nuts and grasses to eat.
Cats hunted too, but mostly by night.
Their paths rarely crossed.

Then something changed. Humans stopped moving from place to place in search of food. Instead, they started to grow their own crops. With the grain came the mice. And with the mice came the cats …

Cats did not step into our homes and hearts overnight. This friendship grew over hundreds, if not thousands, of years. So when, and where, did cats become pets?

Cats are part of the family, but this wasn't always the case.

9

3 Spot the leopard cat

Leopard cats are not related to leopards, but they do look a little like them because of their light fur and black spots. They're much smaller than leopards – about the same size as tall pet cats. These beautiful felines have sandy or ginger fur with white tummies. The length of their coat depends on where they live – leopard cat fur is fluffier in the north, where the **climate** is colder.

Leopard cats usually live alone in the forests of Asia, but they have been known to come close to human houses.

Furry facts

Rats, beware! Leopard cats are excellent hunters. They're usually **nocturnal**, doing most of their hunting at night.

Scientists did experiments on 5,000-year-old cat bones that were discovered in China. The bones were found in a farming village. Why were they there?

Wild cats are usually scared of humans and avoid human villages. Were these cats tame – perhaps even pets?

Elburz Mts

Zagros Mts

AFGHANISTAN

PAKISTAN

The Des

Arabian Sea

Western

INDIAN

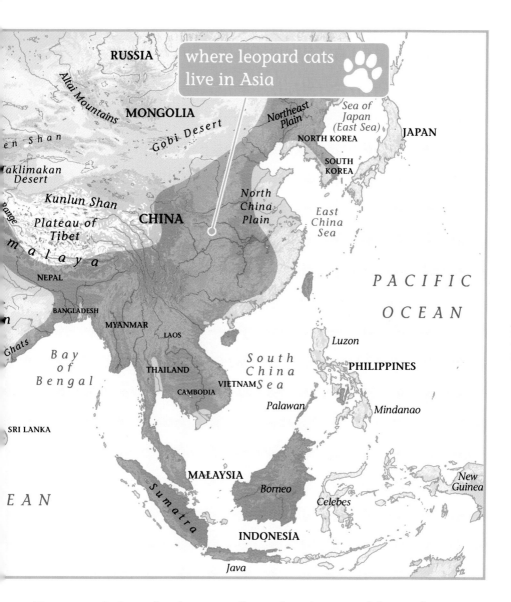

where leopard cats live in Asia

RUSSIA

Altai Mountains

MONGOLIA

Gobi Desert

en shan

Taklimakan Desert

Kunlun Shan

range

Plateau of Tibet

m a l a y a

CHINA

NEPAL

BANGLADESH

n

Ghats

MYANMAR

LAOS

Bay of Bengal

THAILAND

CAMBODIA

SRI LANKA

EAN

Sumatra

Northeast Plain

Sea of Japan (East Sea)

NORTH KOREA

SOUTH KOREA

JAPAN

North China Plain

East China Sea

PACIFIC

OCEAN

Luzon

South China Sea

PHILIPPINES

VIETNAM

Palawan

Mindanao

MALAYSIA

Borneo

Celebes

New Guinea

INDONESIA

Java

By examining the bones, the scientists could see that the cats had eaten rats and mice. They could even tell that the rats and mice had eaten grain!

13

What sort of cats did the bones belong to?
Were they our first pet cats?

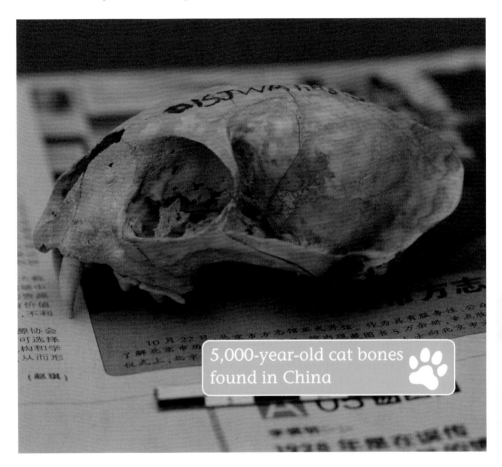

5,000-year-old cat bones found in China

Not leopard cats!

The scientists found that the **ancient** cat bones came from leopard cats. This meant that leopard cats had lived very close to humans. But experiments show that our pet cats are *not* related to leopard cats.

What does this tell us?

Leopard cats in this part of China were probably tame for a while, but then the trail disappears ... It looks like they went wild again!

Bengal cat

Furry facts

Bengals – a **breed** of pet cat – are the result of mixing pet cats with leopard cats. All members of this breed have some leopard cat blood in their veins!

If leopard cats were not the ancestors of our modern pet cats – who were? Our **quest** continues ...

15

4 Born to be wild

Now we know that pet cats did not start off as leopard cats, who are our next furry **suspects**?

Were wildcats the first pet cats? The term "wildcat" means a group of forest and desert felines that are a little larger than our own cats.

Furry facts

Cats have small collarbones that are not attached to their other bones. Together with their bendy spines, this means cats are ultra-flexible like acrobats and allows them to squeeze into narrow places.

Cats are incredibly flexible, which is great for stretching and jumping!

Collarbone: not attached to other bones

Spine: bendy for maximum bounce

Tail: long and flexible to help balance

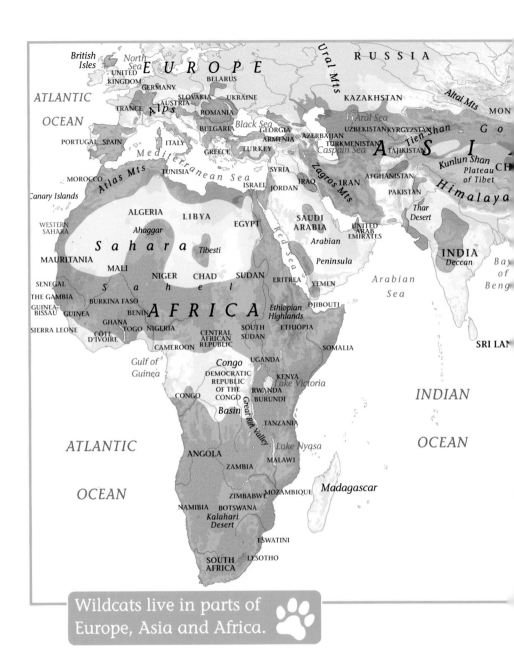

Wildcats live in parts of Europe, Asia and Africa.

There are two main types of wildcat:

- the European wildcat

- the African wildcat.

Wildcats look a lot like tame cats but are a bit larger. European wildcats have thick fur and bushy tails. African wildcats are tall and slim.

5 Wildcats of the woods

European wildcats live in forest **habitats** across Europe, mostly in the northern, cooler parts of the continent.

With their silvery-brown fur and stripes, they look like large tabbies. They're wider and stand a little taller than most pet cats, with fluffier tails.

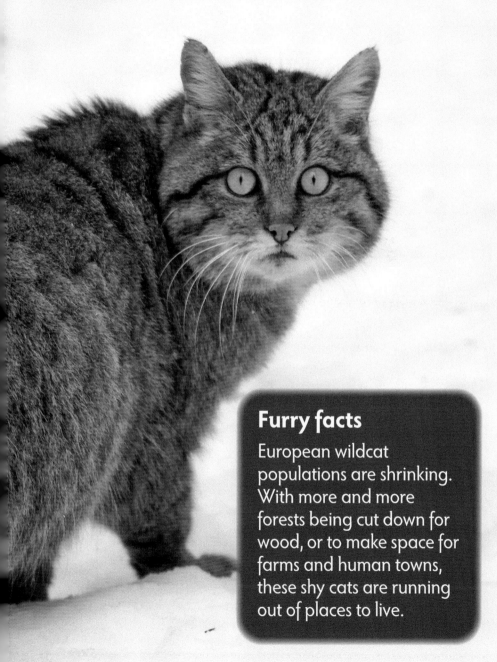

Furry facts

European wildcat populations are shrinking. With more and more forests being cut down for wood, or to make space for farms and human towns, these shy cats are running out of places to live.

Picture *purrfect*

Look at these old paintings from Europe. The cats look like modern kitties – they also look a lot like European wildcats! It isn't surprising that people thought that the first pet cats stepped out of European forests and into our lives. European wildcats *must* be the ancestors of the first pet cats. Right?

Child with Cat by French artist Pierre-Auguste Renoir

Cat and Kittens by English artist Frank Paton

Looks can be deceiving!

Scientists have discovered that *all* pet cats – from Europe to Asia and Africa, through North to South America, and even in Australia – have the same wild ancestor. But they are *not* European wildcats.

So where *did* the first pet cats come from?

6 The Middle East

To solve the puzzle of how cats became our friends, let's go to the place where it all began.

The Middle East is an area of land where the continents of Europe, Asia and Africa meet. A lot of the world's oldest towns were built in the Middle East, and crops were first grown there, near the Mediterranean Sea.

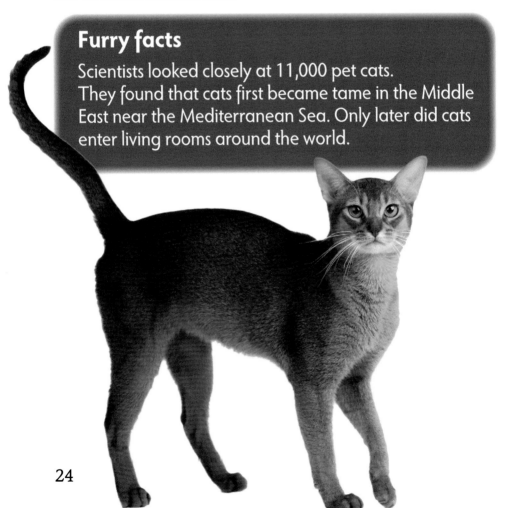

Furry facts

Scientists looked closely at 11,000 pet cats. They found that cats first became tame in the Middle East near the Mediterranean Sea. Only later did cats enter living rooms around the world.

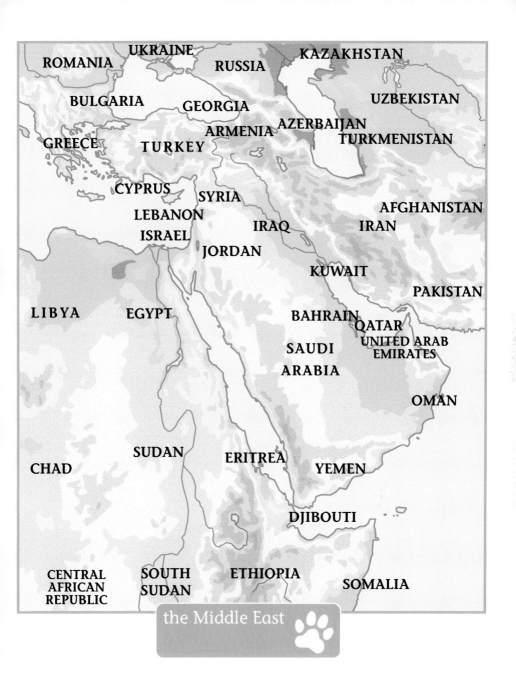

the Middle East

As towns grew along the Mediterranean Sea, people started travelling from place to place, creating trade routes for things like food and clothes. It looks like cats also travelled these routes, hunting the mice that gobbled the grain.

a cat overlooking ancient ruins in Petra, Jordan

How farming made cats come closer

People began to grow grain.
Mice came to nibble the grain.
Cats came to eat the mice.

a cat relaxes by
the Red Sea, Israel

7 The island cat

When were cats tamed?

Ancient cat bones have been discovered on
the island of Cyprus on the Mediterranean Sea.
The cat was buried next to a human 9,500 years ago.
The grave also contained shells, jewellery, tools
and polished stones. Is this the site of the first pet cat?

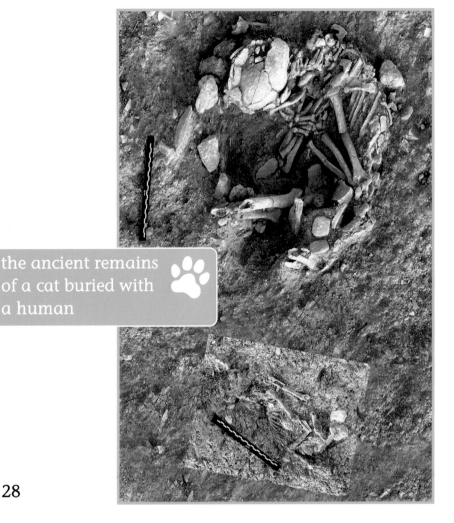

the ancient remains
of a cat buried with
a human

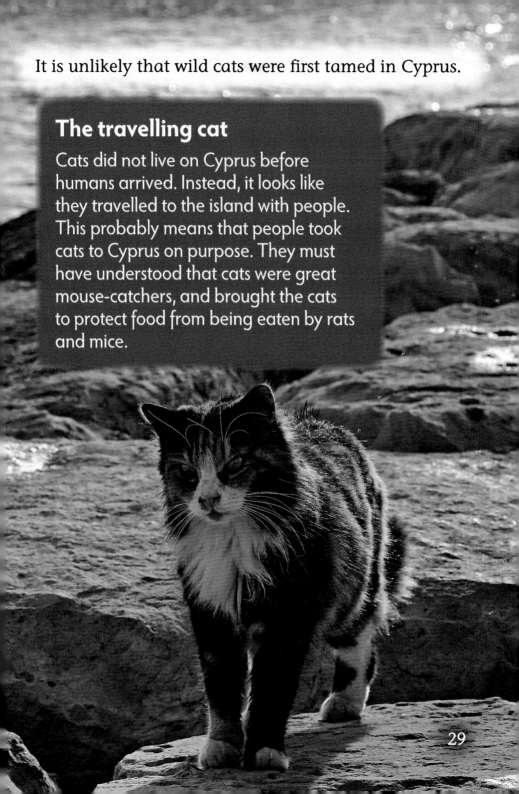

It is unlikely that wild cats were first tamed in Cyprus.

The travelling cat

Cats did not live on Cyprus before humans arrived. Instead, it looks like they travelled to the island with people. This probably means that people took cats to Cyprus on purpose. They must have understood that cats were great mouse-catchers, and brought the cats to protect food from being eaten by rats and mice.

The island cat was buried almost 10,000 years ago! Were cats already our friends then? It's more likely that they lived like some farm cats do now, chasing our mice but not coming into our homes.

farm cats keeping the crops free of **rodents**

Furry facts

Cats' tails help them balance like a tightrope walker's stick. Their tails also tell us how they are feeling.

 Flicking tail: "I'm angry – give me space!"

 Puffy tail: "I'm scared – leave me alone!"

 Raised tail: "I'm happy – let's hang out!"

It is an honour if a cat wraps its tail around you – it's like a feline cuddle.

Cats use their tails to help them balance.

8 Cats of the Nile

5,000-year-old art from Ancient Egypt shows the goddess Bastet with the head of a lioness. 2,000 years later, Bastet was no longer shown as a lioness – she had been **transformed** into a much gentler pet cat.

Bastet was the goddess of childbirth, maybe because cats are so good at having kittens!

Goddess Bastet first **appeared** with the head of a lioness.

Over time, Bastet became a gentler cat.

At Bastet's temple in the Nile Delta, cats roamed about doing much as they pleased. They kept the temple free of mice, sunbathed on its lawn and greeted visitors with purrs. It was a crime to kill a cat; the punishment was death! Is this where the first pet cat was found?

33

Ancient Egyptian cat-lovers

The Ancient Egyptians had special ways of preparing their dead for burial. They mummified them! Dozens of cat mummies were found in the Nile Delta. Mummification was expensive, so the fact that cats were mummified shows they were important.

a mummified cat in Ancient Egypt

What is mummification?

Mummification was the way Ancient Egyptians prepared dead people for the afterlife. The body was wrapped with bandages from head to toe. Once ready, the mummy was put in a large box called a "sarcophagus".

a sarcophagus

9 From hunter to house cat

At about the same time that the goddess Bastet turned into a small cat, we see other changes in Egyptian art. Cats are shown living in houses and wearing collars. Cats were now more than helpful hunters – they had become pets.

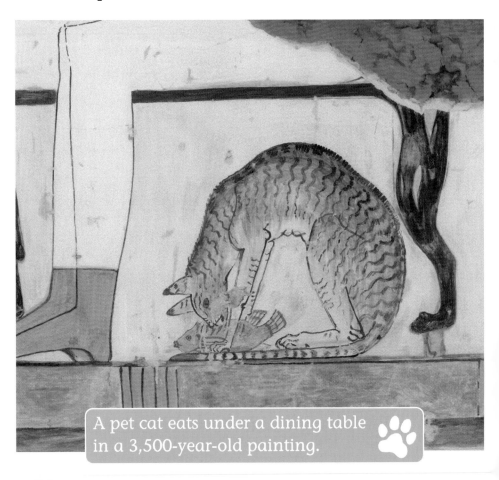

A pet cat eats under a dining table in a 3,500-year-old painting.

The bronze "Gayer-Anderson cat" is one of the best examples of Ancient Egyptian cat sculpture. It shows the goddess Bastet wearing a collar and jewellery.

Scientists looked at the bones and other remains of 200 ancient cats. The results seem to tell us that cats became tame in stages.

Twice tamed

1 Cats came closer to humans with early farming.

🐾 Where? Maybe in Turkey, near Cyprus, where the cat bones were found

🐾 When? Up to 10,000 years ago

2 Slowly, cats moved into our homes.

🐾 Where? In Egypt, the centre of cat worship

🐾 When? About 4,000 years ago

We have discovered where and how cats became our friends. The pieces of the puzzle are finally coming together! But who were the ancestors of pet cats? They weren't leopard cats or European wildcats. It's time to turn to our third suspect, African wildcats …

10 Wildcats of the desert

Stripy African wildcats look like large pet cats. These fierce little hunters live in large parts of Africa, the Middle East and Asia.

Furry facts

African wildcats' amazing eyesight helps them hunt. They are six times better than us at seeing in near darkness! Pet cats have the same super-sight.

Were African wildcats the first pet cats?

Studies show that our pet cats have hardly changed for thousands of years. They are a lot like their ancestors.

The cat's out of the bag!

We now know that ALL pet cats around the world share the same ancestors – African wildcats!

11 Did cats tame themselves?

Cats are different from other tame animals. They remain fierce, often territorial, hunters. They may want to be cuddled, but only if they feel like it. Unlike horses, they will not be led. Unlike dogs, they will not follow commands.

Is it any surprise that these small, clever animals probably tamed themselves? Their natural curiosity brought them near to farms. The chance of food saw cats come closer. Treated kindly, they chose to stay.

Tiger in your living room

In the heart of every pet cat beats the call of the wild. Spotted, striped or fluffy, don't let that sweet face fool you! The cat is tame – but not completely. Hunter, acrobat, free spirit … the tiger in your living room.

A cat is
a free spirit.

Glossary

ancestor a member of a cat's family that lived before it

ancient very old

appeared moved into a place where it could be seen

breed a particular kind of animal

carnivore animal that eats meat

climate the sort of weather a place normally has

domestic not wild/kept as a pet

evidence anything you see, read or are told that gives you reason to believe something is true

fearsome frightening

feline linked to cats

habitats the natural homes of animals or plants

independent to not need help from anyone else

majestic like a king or queen

nocturnal active at night

prehistoric a long time ago, before history was written down

quest a search for something

rodents animals such as mice or rats

solitary on your own

suspects people (or animals!) who may have done something

transformed changed

Index

Where did our pet cats come from?

Leopard cat
* Spotted like a leopard
* Excellent hunter
* Last seen near Chinese farms

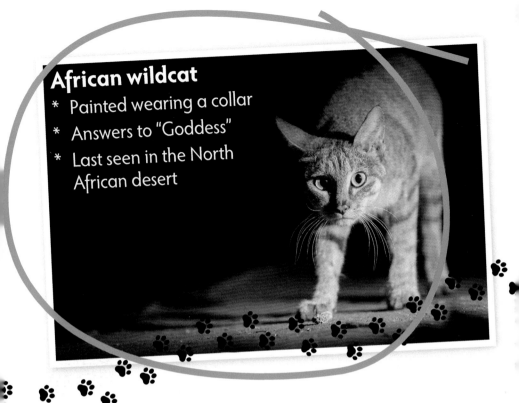

African wildcat

* Painted wearing a collar
* Answers to "Goddess"
* Last seen in the North African desert

European wildcat

* Fluffy and stripy
* Like cats in old paintings
* Last seen in European woods

Ideas for reading

Written by Christine Whitney
Primary Literacy Consultant

Reading objectives:
- be introduced to non-fiction books that are structured in different ways
- listen to, discuss and express views about non-fiction
- retrieve and record information from non-fiction
- discuss and clarify the meanings of words

Spoken language objectives:
- participate in discussion
- speculate, hypothesise, imagine and explore ideas through talk
- ask relevant questions

Curriculum links: Science: Identify and name a variety of common animals that are carnivores; Writing: Write for different purposes

Word count: 2540

Interest words: carnivores, domestic, habitats, rodents, nocturnal

Resources: Paper and pencils

Build a context for reading

- Ask the group if anyone has a cat. Encourage children to share brief descriptions of their cat, including its name.
- Before the children see the book, read the title to them *Tiger in your Living Room*. Ask children to make predictions about the content of the book.
- Now show the cover and read the blurb on the back cover. Take answers to the question, *How did these brave little hunters become our friends?*
- Introduce the words *carnivores, domestic, habitats, rodents, nocturnal*. Ask children to work in pairs to suggest a sentence which uses one of these words correctly. Check understanding of correct usage.

Understand and apply reading strategies

- Turn to the contents page and read through the different sections in the book. Ask for volunteers to say which section they are most interested in reading and why.